# SUPER-EASY STEP-BY-STEP SAUSAGEMAKING

Other Books by Yvonne Young Tarr

The Ten Minute Gourmet Cookbook
The Ten Minute Gourmet Diet Cookbook
101 Desserts to Make You Famous
Love Portions
The New York Times Natural Foods Dieting Book
The Complete Outdoor Cookbook
The New York Times Bread and Soup Cookbook
The Farmhouse Cookbook
Super-Easy Step-by-Step Cheesemaking
Super-Easy Step-by-Step Winemaking
Super-Easy Step-by-Step Book of Special Breads
The Up-with-Wholesome, Down-with-Storebought
Book of Recipes and Household Formulas

# SUPER-EASY STEP-BY-STEP SAUSAGEMAKING

## YVONNE YOUNG TARR

Vintage Books
A Division of Random House, Inc.
New York

VINTAGE BOOKS EDITION 1975

Copyright © 1975 by Yvonne Young Tarr

All rights reserved under International and
Pan-American Copyright Conventions.
Published in the United States by Random
House, Inc., New York, and simultaneously
in Canada by Random House of Canada
Limited, Toronto.

Manufactured in the United States of America

**Library of Congress Cataloging in Publication Data**
Tarr, Yvonne Young.
Super-easy step-by-step sausagemaking book.

1. Sausages. 2. Cookery (Sausages) I. Title
TX749.T26   641.6'6   75-13619
ISBN 0-394-72011-3

# INTRODUCTION

Sausages . . . round, fat, sizzling and sputtering in the pan. Sausages broiling to a golden turn. Sausages smoked to a dark mahogany. Sausages long, sausages midget-size, sausages as thin as your finger or as thick as your arm. Sausages succulent and soft as butter. Dried sausages hard as wood and reeking with garlic. Italian sausages hot enough to bring tears to your eyes. German sausages subtle and white with just a touch of herbs. Far from just scraps and undesirable parts of animals stuffed into casings, sausages, generally made from choice cuts, are the aristocrats of meats.

From generation to generation, successful sausagemakers have kept from the world their secret recipes—their spice lists, what meats they combined, what proportions they used. And little wonder . . . one sausage company paid a retiring sausagemaker $25,000 for the privilege of sharing his secret, because they knew that there is only one ingredient that really makes the difference in sausagemaking—a good recipe. This book gives you that essential ingredient. These recipes have been painstakingly collected from farm kitchens, English pubs, generous sausagemakers and medieval receipt books. Each has been meticulously tested and retested to insure that the sausages you make will compare favorably with the best sold anywhere—from farmer's markets to German sausage stores.

There are many advantages to making your own sausages.

First, the homemade variety tastes better. Second, you flavor the meat to suit your taste and use the kinds of meat and amounts of fat you prefer. Third, the sausages you make yourself may be made without dangerous preservatives, from high-quality ingredients as fresh and sanitary as you choose to make them. And last, but in these times surely not least, own-made sausages are money-saving meal stretchers. Sausages take naturally to extension with wholesome fillers such as oatmeal, soy beans or, in a pinch, bread crumbs. There are even a few sausage recipes that feature vegetables. Experiment with all of these, and then, since sausages freeze well, stock your freezer with the ones you like best.

# HOW TO MAKE THIS BOOK WORK FOR YOU

Sausagemaking is not difficult, but you may find it helpful to acquaint yourself with the basic procedures before beginning. These are clearly outlined in the back of the book and are referred to (with page numbers) throughout the text of each recipe.

# Contents

Introduction                                          V

How to Make This Book Work for You     VI

The Sausagemaking Process Simplified     1
Sausagemaking Simplified                      2

Equipment                                            5
Basic Equipment List                             6
Description of Sausagemaking Equipment     6

Recipes                                              9
Economy Sausages                              10
Sausages with Oatmeal                         10
Gruetz Wurst                                     13
Pork and Soybean Sausages                  16
Swedish Potato Sausage (Potatis Korv)     19
Scrapple or Ponhaws                           22
Homemade Breakfast Pork Sausage          24
Smoked Country Sausage                      26
Homemade German Bratwurst                29
Liver Sausage                                    32
Vienna Sausage                                  35
Homemade Polish-Style Sausage
   (Kielbasa)                                      38
Italian-Style Sausage                           41
Chicken Sausage                                43

Head Cheese 46

**Recipes with Sausage** 49
Bubble and Squeak 50
Toad in the Hole 52
Poor Man's Paella 54
Italian Sausage Casserole 56
Sausage Baked in Italian Bread 58
Deep-Fried Sausage Pies 60
    Sausage and Potato Filling 61
    Sausage and Egg Filling 61
    Vienna Sausage Filling 61
Midwestern Boiled Dinner 62
Sausage and Potato Salad 63
Pie Crust 65
White Sauce 66
Vinaigrette Sauce 67

**The Process Described** 69
Chopping or Grinding the Meat 70
Mixing the Ingredients 70
Preparing and Storing the Casings 71
Shaping the Meat 73
Filling the Casings 74
Tying Off 77
Smoking the Sausages 77
Storing Sausages 78
Cooking the Sausage 79

# THE SAUSAGEMAKING PROCESS SIMPLIFIED

# SAUSAGEMAKING SIMPLIFIED

The sausagemaking process basically consists of the following steps:

1 . . . chopping or grinding the meat
2 . . . mixing the ingredients
3 . . . preparing the casings
4 . . . shaping the sausage into patties or rolls, or stuffing it into casings and tying off
5 . . . smoking or precooking the sausages (for smoked sausages only)
6 . . . storing the sausages
7 . . . cooking the sausages

# EQUIPMENT

# BASIC EQUIPMENT LIST

Chopping knife and board, *or*
A meat grinder
Mixing bowl
Large funnel, *or*
Sausage stuffing nozzle
Wooden spoon
Natural casings, *or*
Muslin casings

# DESCRIPTION OF SAUSAGEMAKING EQUIPMENT

**Chopping Knife and Board:** for hand chopping meat, *or*

**A Meat Grinder:** either electric or hand-operated, with a coarse (large-holed) disk

**Mixing Bowl:** for combining ingredients

**Large Funnel:** for filling casings by hand, *or*

**Sausage Stuffing Nozzle:** a convenient but nonessential attachment, available for some electric and hand grinders

**Wooden Spoon:** for mixing and for forcing sausage mixture through funnel into casings

**Natural Casings:** for stuffing sausages; usually salted and packed dry for easy storage, and available in a variety of widths for making sausages of varying thickness, *or*

**Muslin Casings:** sewed from strips of plain unbleached muslin according to size desired

# RECIPES

# ECONOMY SAUSAGES

The extension of sausage meats with grains and soybeans actually enhances rather than diminishes the flavor. People will never guess that these sausages are not 100-percent meat unless you tell them. Since you control the amount of fat in the sausage, they're great for anyone who is on a diet — or a budget.

# SAUSAGES WITH OATMEAL

Serve this mild sausage for breakfast, lunch or dinner.
(Yield: 24 link sausages)

## INGREDIENTS

2 Pounds pork tenderloin
½ Pound veal
1½ Pounds *fresh* pork fat
2 Cups rolled oats
1 Cup water
1 Tablespoon salt
1 Teaspoon caraway seeds
⅛ Teaspoon each ground allspice and ginger

## EQUIPMENT

All equipment listed in Basic Equipment List, page 6.

## STEP ONE
## CHOPPING OR GRINDING THE MEAT

Chop meat and fat into ¼-inch dice or force through large disk of grinder (*see* Chopping or Grinding the Meat, page 70).

## STEP TWO
# PRECOOKING AND MIXING THE INGREDIENTS

**A.** Place rolled oats and water in a saucepan and bring to a boil.

---

**B.** Drain immediately and cool in the refrigerator for 15 minutes.

---

**C.** Mix meat, fat, oats, salt, caraway seeds, allspice and ginger (*see* Mixing, page 70).

## STEP THREE
## FILLING THE CASINGS

Force the mixture into soaked and rinsed natural casings (*see* Preparing and Storing the Casings, page 71), using either funnel and spoon or grinder method (*see* Filling the Casings, page 74).

## STEP FOUR
## TYING OFF

Twist or tie off the casings in links of desired length (*see* Tying Off, page 77).

## STEP FIVE
# STORING THE SAUSAGE

Sausage must be quickly and properly stored to prevent spoilage (*see* Storing Sausages, page 78).

## STEP SIX
# COOKING THE SAUSAGE

This is a nice, mild sausage that goes well with eggs in the morning, pancakes for lunch or spaghetti for dinner. Follow directions for cooking sausages, page 79.

# GRUETZ WURST

A leaner version of oatmeal/meat sausage, this pork and beef combination freezes extremely well.
(Yield: about 7 pounds)

## INGREDIENTS

4 Pounds pork shoulder, cut into 1-inch pieces
2 Pounds stewing beef or ground beef
3 Cups uncooked oatmeal
3 Onions, chopped
2 Tablespoons butter
1 Tablespoon powdered sage
¼ Teaspoon ground allspice
Salt and pepper to taste

## EQUIPMENT

All equipment listed in Basic Equipment List, page 6.

## STEP ONE
## PREPARING THE INGREDIENTS

**A.** Cook meats together in water to cover until very tender.

**B.** Prepare oatmeal according to package directions and cook until very thick.

**C.** Sauté chopped onions in the butter until soft and transparent.

## STEP TWO
# CHOPPING THE MEAT

Cut meats into ¼-inch dice or grind coarsely (*see* Chopping or Grinding the Meat, page 70).

## STEP THREE
# MIXING THE INGREDIENTS

**A.** Combine meats with oatmeal and onions. Mix thoroughly.

---

**B.** Add sage and allspice, then season to taste with salt and pepper (*see* Mixing the Ingredients, page 70).

## STEP FOUR
# FILLING THE CASINGS

Force mixture into soaked and rinsed natural casings or muslin casings (*see* Preparing and Storing the Casings, page 71), using either funnel and spoon or grinder method (*see* Filling the Casings, page 74).

## STEP FIVE
# TYING OFF

Tie off in 5-inch lengths (*see* Tying Off, page 77).

## STEP SIX
# PRECOOKING THE SAUSAGE

**A.** Put sausages in deep kettle, add water to cover and bring to just under a boil.

**B.** Allow to simmer, covered, for about 40 minutes. Drain.

## STEP SEVEN
# STORING THE SAUSAGE

Sausage must be quickly and properly stored to prevent spoilage (*see* Storing the Sausage, page 78). Eat cold or reheat in water.

# PORK AND SOYBEAN SAUSAGES

These sausages have an interesting texture and a fine nutty flavor.

(Yield: about 4½ pounds)

## INGREDIENTS
2 Pounds pork tenderloin
½ Pound smoked pork butt
1½ Pounds fresh pork fat
1½ Cups soybeans
1 Cup water
1 Tablespoon salt
⅛ Teaspoon each ground nutmeg and allspice

## EQUIPMENT
All equipment listed in Basic Equipment List, page 6.

## STEP ONE
## CHOPPING OR GRINDING THE MEAT

Chop the meat and fat into ¼-inch dice or force through the large disk of your grinder (see Chopping or Grinding the Meat, page 70).

## STEP TWO
## PRECOOKING AND MIXING THE INGREDIENTS

A. Place soybeans in the water, bring to a boil and boil for 5 minutes.

**B.** Drain the beans and chop or grind them into ⅛-inch pieces.

**C.** Cool to room temperature.

**D.** Use your fingers to knead together the meats, fat, beans, salt and spices (*see* Mixing, page 70).

## STEP THREE
## SHAPING THE SAUSAGE

Form into patties or stuff into soaked and rinsed natural casings, using either funnel and spoon or grinder (*see* Filling the Casings, page 74).

## STEP FOUR
## TYING OFF

Twist the casings or tie off in desired lengths (*see* Tying Off, page 77).

## STEP FIVE
## STORING THE SAUSAGE

This sausage, as all sausages, must be quickly and properly stored to prevent spoilage (*see* Storing Sausages, page 78).

# STEP SIX
# COOKING THE SAUSAGE

Serve this sausage in patties or links, alone, with sauerkraut and mashed potatoes, or in any other sausage recipe. (It also makes delicious stuffing for any fowl because of its crunchy, nutlike flavor.)

Follow directions for cooking given in Cooking the Sausages, page 79.

# SWEDISH POTATO SAUSAGE (POTATIS KORV)

Potato sausage, or *Potatis Korv,* a traditional sausage prepared in the Swedish province of Varmland, is particularly popular at Christmas time.

(Yield: 9 pounds)

## INGREDIENTS

2 Pounds round steak
2 Pounds pork shoulder
8 Large potatoes
½ Teaspoon white pepper
1½ Teaspoons dry mustard
¼ Teaspoon each ground allspice and ground nutmeg
2 Medium onions, peeled
1 Tablespoon salt (or more to taste)
Cold water as needed
Natural pork casings
1 Tablespoon whole allspice (used in boiling)

## EQUIPMENT

All equipment listed in Basic Equipment List, page 6.

## STEP ONE
## CHOPPING OR GRINDING THE MEAT

Mince the meats very finely with a sharp knife, or grind them separately twice and then once again together, using the fine disk of your grinder.

## STEP TWO
# PRECOOKING AND MIXING THE INGREDIENTS

**A.** Peel and parboil potatoes. Cool.

**B.** Finely chop potatoes and onions with a sharp knife, or grind together, using fine disk of grinder.

**C.** Mix potatoes, onions and meats together with a large wooden spoon. Add seasonings and mix again.

**D.** Add enough cold water to soften the mixture. Knead well with your hands (*see* Mixing the Ingredients, page 70).

**E.** Test consistency and taste by frying a small sample — you may prefer your sausage more highly spiced. If so, add more seasonings.

## STEP THREE
# FILLING THE CASINGS

**A.** Stuff mixture rather loosely into 24-inch soaked and rinsed natural casings (*see* Preparing and Storing the Casings, page 71), using either the funnel and spoon or grinder method (*see* Filling the Casings, page 74).

**B.** Prick with a large needle if any air bubbles form.

## STEP FOUR
## TYING OFF

Fill two 24-inch casings and tie the ends of each together to form rings.

## STEP FIVE
## STORING THE SAUSAGE

Store sausage quickly and properly to prevent spoilage (*see* Storing Sausages, page 78).

## STEP SIX
## COOKING THE SAUSAGE

**A.** To cook, boil for 45 minutes in a kettle large enough to prevent crowding. Add whole allspice to cooking water.

**B.** Remove froth as it accumulates.

**C.** Cut rings into 2-inch slices. Serve hot or cold.

# SCRAPPLE OR PONHAWS

This old-fashioned treat is not a sausage, but it is prepared from minced meats and is such a money-saver that it really deserves a place in this collection.

(Yield: 3 pounds)

## INGREDIENTS

2 Pounds pork shoulder
¼ Pound liver
5 Cups water
1⅓ Cups yellow cornmeal
2 Teaspoons salt
1 Medium onion, minced
1¼ Teaspoons each powdered marjoram and sage
½ Teaspoon leaf thyme
Dash ground cloves

## EQUIPMENT

Large, sharp knife
Saucepan
Loaf pan

## STEP ONE
## PREPARING THE MEATS

**A.** Place pork and liver in a deep saucepan, add 4 cups water, and cook over medium heat for 1 hour.

**B.** Drain the meats and reserve the cooking liquid.

**C.** Use a sharp knife to mince the meats.

## STEP TWO
# MIXING AND COOKING THE INGREDIENTS

**A.** Mix cornmeal and salt in a large saucepan. Stir in 2 cups reserved cooking liquid and remaining cup water.

---

**B.** Cook over medium-low heat, stirring constantly, until mixture is very thick.

---

**C.** Stir in meat, onions, marjoram, sage, thyme and cloves.

---

**D.** Reduce heat to very low and simmer the mixture, covered, for about 1 hour, stirring occasionally.

## STEP THREE
# FORMING THE LOAF

Pour mixture into a loaf pan, allow to cool slightly, then refrigerate.

## STEP FOUR
# COOKING

To serve, cut the chilled loaf into ⅓-inch slices, sauté the slices in butter until golden brown on both sides and serve hot with maple syrup.

# HOMEMADE BREAKFAST PORK SAUSAGE

To make this breakfast pork sausage, add sage with a heavy hand for that country-kitchen taste. For a spicy sausage, add ⅛ teaspoon cayenne.

(Yield: about 2½ pounds)

### INGREDIENTS

2½ Pounds pork (about 80% lean)
2½ Teaspoons powdered sage
1½ Teaspoons marjoram
½ Teaspoon savory
2 Teaspoons salt
2 Teaspoons ground black pepper
¼ Teaspoon ground nutmeg
¼ Cup warm water

### EQUIPMENT

All equipment listed in Basic Equipment List, page 6

## STEP ONE
## CHOPPING OR GRINDING THE MEAT

Cut pork and fat into ¼-inch dice (*see* Chopping or Grinding the Meat, page 70).

## STEP TWO
## MIXING THE INGREDIENTS

Mix spices with the warm water and work thoroughly into the meat, using your hands to knead the mixture (*see* Mixing the Ingredients, page 70).

## STEP THREE
# SHAPING THE MEAT

Form into patties or rolls (*see* Shaping the Meat, page 73) or stuff into natural casings to make links (*see* Filling the Casings, page 74).

## STEP FOUR
# TYING OFF

If sausage meat is being formed into links, tie off in 4-inch lengths (*see* Tying Off, page 77).

## STEP FIVE
# STORING THE SAUSAGE

Sausage must be quickly and properly stored to prevent spoilage (*see* Storing Sausages, page 78).

## STEP SIX
# COOKING THE SAUSAGE

Follow directions for cooking your sausage patties, rolls or links given in Cooking the Sausage, page 79. Serve hot with eggs, pancakes or French toast.

# SMOKED COUNTRY SAUSAGE

Smoking gives country sausage a particularly interesting flavor.

(Yield: about 7½ pounds)

## INGREDIENTS

7 Pounds lean pork
½ Pound lean beef
2½ Ounces pickling spice
1 Tablespoon black pepper
1 Teaspoon each cayenne pepper, mace, marjoram and sage
Red wine or water

## EQUIPMENT

All equipment listed in Basic Equipment List, page 6.
*Plus*
Sausage smoker

## STEP ONE
## CHOPPING OR GRINDING THE MEAT

Chop meats into ¼-inch dice or force through coarse disk of grinder (*see* Chopping or Grinding the Meat, page 70).

## STEP TWO
## MIXING THE INGREDIENTS

**A.** Blend meats together with spices and seasonings until well mixed.

**B.** Force mixture through fine blade of grinder 3 or 4 times. Pack into any non-metal container and refrigerate for 24 hours.

## STEP THREE
## FILLING THE CASINGS

**A.** Combine sausage mixture with a little red wine or water (see Shaping the Sausage Meat, page 73).

**B.** Stuff into the size casing you prefer and tie off at appropriate lengths (see Tying Off, page 77).

## STEP FOUR
## SMOKING THE SAUSAGES

**A.** Hang the sausages and smoke at 60 degrees F. for 2 hours (see Smoking the Sausages, page 77).

**B.** Increase density of smoke and continue smoking until sausages turn a rich mahogany-brown color. Take care that smokehouse temperature remains below 100 degrees F.

## STEP FIVE
## STORING THE SAUSAGE

Cool the smoked sausages and refrigerate until needed.

Sausage must be quickly and properly stored to prevent spoilage (*see* Storing Sausages, page 78).

## STEP SIX
# COOKING THE SAUSAGE

Cook the sausage according to directions given on page 79.

# HOMEMADE GERMAN BRATWURST

Germany is called the sausage capital of the world, and this bratwurst (meaning "sausage for frying") is a favorite German sausage. Grill these over an open fire, on your charcoal grill or in your broiler, or skillet-fry them and serve with German mustard, cabbage or kraut, rye bread and beer.
(Yield: 3½ pounds)

## INGREDIENTS
2 Pounds lean pork (preferably loin)
1½ Pounds lean veal
½ Teaspoon whole marjoram
½ Teaspoon caraway seeds
½ Teaspoon ground nutmeg
2 Teaspoons salt
1 Teaspoon white pepper
About ¾ cup cold water

## EQUIPMENT
All equipment listed in Basic Equipment List, page 6.

## STEP ONE
## CHOPPING OR GRINDING THE MEAT

Mince the meats with a very sharp knife, or grind them together twice using the *fine* blade of your meat grinder or food chopper (*see* Chopping or Grinding the Meat, page 70).

## STEP TWO
# MIXING THE INGREDIENTS

Combine marjoram, caraway seeds and nutmeg in a mortar and grind to a fine powder with a pestle. Add to the meat along with salt, pepper and water. Mix well (*see* Mixing the Ingredients, page 70).

## STEP THREE
# FILLING THE CASINGS

Force the mixture into soaked and rinsed natural casings (*see* Preparing and Storing the Casings, page 71) using either the funnel and spoon or grinder method (*see* Filling the Casings, page 74).

## STEP FOUR
# TYING OFF

Twist the casings several times at 3- to 4-inch intervals (*see* Tying Off, page 77).

## STEP FIVE
# STORING THE SAUSAGE

Store sausage quickly and properly to prevent spoilage (*see* Storing Sausages, page 78).

## STEP SIX
# COOKING THE SAUSAGE

**A.** To precook, pierce links on both sides with a fork. Partially cover with water, bring to a boil, reduce heat and simmer about 3 minutes. Turn over and simmer 3 minutes more. Drain.

---

**B.** To pan-fry after simmering, add a little oil or butter to skillet, then brown sausage links on all sides, turning frequently, for 10 to 20 minutes.

---

**C.** To grill after simmering, brush links with melted butter or oil. Grill or broil about 5 inches from heat source, turning and brushing with butter frequently, for 10 to 20 minutes.

---

**D.** For a special treat, brown simmered links in butter, then add ale to cover. Cook over low heat, covered, for 20 to 30 minutes. Uncover and cook over high heat until ale is reduced by half. Add sautéed onion, season to taste, then thicken with flour before serving.

# LIVER SAUSAGE

Liver sausages have a hearty, distinctive flavor, best brought out by serving with fried onions and mashed or fried potatoes.

(Yield: about 6 pounds)

## INGREDIENTS

4½ Pounds lean pork or pork scraps (heart, tongue, kidney, etc.)
8 Cups water
1½ Pounds pork liver (or other)
3 Tablespoons salt
1 Tablespoon powdered sage
1 Teaspoon pepper
1 Teaspoon ground allspice
¼ Teaspoon cayenne pepper

## EQUIPMENT

All equipment listed in Basic Equipment List, page 6.

## STEP ONE
## PRELIMINARY COOKING

**A.** Cut pork into 2-inch dice. Place in kettle and cover with 8 cups water. Cook over medium heat for about one hour, or until tender.

**B.** Cut liver into 1-inch strips. Add to kettle and cook along with pork for 30 minutes longer, or until liver is tender.

## STEP TWO
# CHOPPING OR GRINDING THE MEAT

**A.** Drain meats and reserve broth.

**B.** Cut meats into ¼-inch dice or grind medium fine (*see* Chopping or Grinding the Meat, page 70).

## STEP THREE
# MIXING THE INGREDIENTS

Add 1 cup reserved cooking broth and seasonings to chopped or ground meats. Mix thoroughly. (*Note*: Remaining broth may be used for soup stock.)

## STEP FOUR
# FILLING THE CASINGS

Grind meat mixture once more and stuff into wide natural casings from 1½ to 4 inches in diameter (*see* Preparing and Storing the Casings, page 71).

## STEP FIVE
# TYING OFF

Tie off at 7- to 8-inch intervals (*see* Tying Off, page 77).

## STEP SIX
# COOKING THE SAUSAGE

**A.** Put sausage in a deep kettle, add water to cover, and bring to just under a boil. Reduce heat and simmer sausages for 30 minutes, or until they float to surface.

**B.** Drain sausages, then plunge into cold water. When cool, hang to dry in a cool place.

## STEP SEVEN
# STORING THE SAUSAGE

Sausage must be quickly and properly stored to prevent spoilage (*see* Storing the Sausages, page 78).

# VIENNA SAUSAGE

Tie off tasty Vienna sausage in different lengths and widths to make the sausage you like best. This versatile mixture makes 3-inch midget Vienna sausages, 5-inch wieners, or fat, sturdy frankfurters depending on the width of the casing you use. Serve them cold or reheat at serving time.

(Yield: about 6 pounds)

## INGREDIENTS

2 Pounds lean beef
2 Pounds lean pork
2 Pounds fat pork
1 Cup all-purpose flour
3 Tablespoons salt
4 Tablespoons ground coriander
1¼ Teaspoons ground mace
¾ Teaspoon cayenne pepper
1½ Teaspoons granulated sugar
1 Teaspoon saltpeter
¼ Cup minced onion
2¼ Cups cold water

## EQUIPMENT

All equipment listed in Basic Equipment List, page 6.
*Plus*
Sausage smoker

# STEP ONE
# CHOPPING OR GRINDING THE MEAT

Cut the meats into ¼-inch dice or grind coarsely (*see* Chopping or Grinding the Meat, page 70).

## STEP TWO
# MIXING THE INGREDIENTS

**A.** Combine flour with spices, sugar and saltpeter. Sift together and add to meats.

**B.** Stir onion and water into meat mixture. Mix thoroughly.

## STEP THREE
# FILLING THE CASINGS

Put meat mixture through fine blade of grinder and force into soaked and rinsed natural casings or muslin casings (*see* Preparing and Storing the Casings, page 71).

## STEP FOUR
# TYING OFF

Use the size casing you prefer and tie off at appropriate lengths (*see* Tying Off, page 77).

## STEP FIVE
# SMOKING THE SAUSAGE

Hang the sausages and allow them to smoke for 4 to 5 hours, or until rich toasty brown (*see* Smoking the Sausages, page 77).

## STEP SIX
# PRECOOKING THE SAUSAGE

**A.** Put sausages in a deep kettle, add water to cover, and bring to just under a boil. Reduce heat and simmer the sausages for 10 minutes, or until they float to surface.

**B.** Drain sausages, then plunge into cold water. When cool, hang up to dry.

## STEP SEVEN
# STORING THE SAUSAGE

Refrigerate until needed.

## STEP EIGHT
# COOKING THE SAUSAGES

Bring water to a boil, lower the heat, add the sausages and simmer for 10 minutes.

# HOMEMADE POLISH-STYLE SAUSAGE (KIELBASA)

The Polish favorite, kielbasa, is one of the few sausages made with beef. There are as many versions of this sausage as there are Polish sausagemakers, but most use meat blended with marjoram, sage and garlic. Some kielbasa is cooked fresh, some is smoked; both varieties are usually served with kapusta, or sauerkraut.

(Yield: about 3 pounds)

## INGREDIENTS

2¼ Pounds pork butt (about 80% lean), cut into 2-inch chunks
¾ Pound fairly lean beef also cut into chunks
1 Medium onion, peeled
2 Cloves garlic, peeled
Fat or oil
3 Teaspoons whole marjoram
1 Teaspoon powdered sage
1 Teaspoon thyme
2 Bay leaves
⅓ Cup warm water
2 Teaspoons salt
2 Teaspoons peppercorns, coarsely crushed
½ Teaspoon ground nutmeg

## EQUIPMENT

All equipment listed in Basic Equipment List, page 6.

## STEP ONE

## CHOPPING OR GRINDING THE MEAT

Cut meats into ¼-inch dice (*see* Chopping or Grinding the Meats, page 70).

## STEP TWO
# MIXING THE INGREDIENTS

**A.** Chop onion and mince garlic. Add fat or oil to a small skillet and lightly sauté onion, garlic and marjoram. Add sage, thyme, bay leaves and warm water. Stir, then simmer for 2 minutes. Let mixture stand, covered, about 10 minutes. Remove bay leaves.

---

**B.** Add skillet mixture to chopped or ground meats along with salt, crushed peppercorns and nutmeg. Mix well (*see* Mixing the Ingredients, page 70). Knead mixture well with your hands, then chop or grind again.

## STEP THREE
# FILLING THE CASINGS

Force mixture into soaked and rinsed natural casings (*see* Preparing and the Storing Casings, page 71), using either the funnel and spoon or grinder method (*see* Filling the Casings, page 74).

## STEP FOUR
# TYING OFF

Tie off in 5-inch lengths (*see* Tying Off, page 77).

## STEP FIVE
# STORING THE SAUSAGE

Sausage must be quickly and properly stored to prevent spoilage (*see* Storing Sausages, page 78).

## STEP SIX
# COOKING THE SAUSAGE

To cook, simmer slowly in water to cover for 15 minutes. Drain well. Broil to brown all sides. Serve with sauerkraut simmered with chopped tomatoes in the traditional Polish manner.

# ITALIAN-STYLE SAUSAGE

If you like your sausage highly spiced, this recipe is sure to please you.

(Yield: about 3 pounds)

## INGREDIENTS

2½ Pounds lean pork
½ Pound lean beef
1 Pound *fresh* pork fat
10 Large cloves garlic, peeled
2 Teaspoons crushed red pepper
2 Teaspoons fennel seed, slightly crushed
1 Teaspoon thyme leaves
4 Bay leaves, finely crumbled
2 Teaspoons salt
1 Tablespoon whole black pepper
¼ Teaspoon ground nutmeg

## EQUIPMENT

All equipment listed in Basic Equipment List, page 6.

## STEP ONE
## CHOPPING OR GRINDING THE MEAT

Cut meat and fat into ¼-inch dice (*see* Chopping or Grinding the Meat, page 70).

## STEP TWO
## MIXING THE INGREDIENTS

**A.** Mince the garlic.

B. Work all ingredients together (*see* Mixing the Ingredients, page 70).

## STEP THREE
# SHAPING THE SAUSAGE

Shape into patties or rolls (see Shaping the Meat, page 73), or stuff into natural casings for link sausages (see Filling the Casings, page 74).

## STEP FOUR
# TYING OFF

If sausage is being formed into links, tie off in 4- to 5-inch lengths (see Tying Off, page 77).

## STEP FIVE
# STORING THE SAUSAGE

Sausage must be quickly and properly stored to prevent spoilage (see Storing Sausages, page 78).

## STEP SIX
# COOKING THE SAUSAGE

Follow directions for cooking your sausage patties, rolls or links given in Cooking the Sausage, page 79.

# CHICKEN SAUSAGE

One of the easiest sausages to make, chicken sausage need not be stuffed into casings, but merely wrapped in cheesecloth and cooked in stock. The delicate flavor and fine texture make it an unbelievably tasty sandwich filler. (This sausage does not freeze well.)

(Yield: 1 sausage about 15 inches long)

### INGREDIENTS
2 Pounds cooked white meat chicken
½ Pound boiled ham
Chicken bones or 6 chicken bouillon cubes
⅓ Pound chicken livers
6 Eggs
½ Teaspoon salt
⅛ Teaspoon each ground nutmeg and pepper
2 Tablespoons brandy (optional)
3 Cups cracker crumbs

### EQUIPMENT
Meat grinder, sharp knife for chopping, large bowl, spoon, measuring spoons, wire whisk (or eggbeater), cheesecloth.

## STEP ONE
## GRINDING THE MEAT AND COOKING THE STOCK

**A.** Force chicken and ham through the fine blade of meat grinder.

**B.** Put chicken bones or bouillon cubes up to boil in 5 quarts water and 5 tablespoons salt.

## STEP TWO
# MIXING THE INGREDIENTS

**A.** Boil chicken livers for 6 minutes in water to cover. Drain well and mince.

---

**B.** Beat 4 eggs, salt, nutmeg, pepper and brandy into the minced livers.

---

**C.** Stir the ground meats into the liver and eggs along with enough cracker crumbs to make a sausage mixture firm enough to shape into a roll.

## STEP THREE
# FORMING THE SAUSAGE

**A.** Turn the sausage mixture onto wax paper and shape into a roll about 3 inches thick and 15 inches long.

---

**B.** Roll the sausage in bread crumbs to cover (don't forget the ends of the sausage).

---

**C.** Beat the remaining eggs in a baking dish long enough to hold the sausage.

**D.** Roll the sausage in the beaten egg, then once again in cracker crumbs.

**E.** Repeat Step *D* above.

## STEP FOUR
## COOKING THE SAUSAGE

**A.** Roll the sausage in a piece of cheesecloth long enough to wrap around it at least three times.

**B.** Tie off the ends with strong string.

**C.** Cook the sausage (in the cheesecloth) in the broth (*see* Step One B) at a low boil for 1½ hours.

## STEP FIVE
## STORING THE SAUSAGE

**A.** Remove sausage from cooking liquid and cool at room temperature for 8 hours.

**B.** Refrigerate for 24 hours before using. Keep refrigerated.

# HEAD CHEESE (WITH OR WITHOUT THE HEAD)

Head cheese is not cheese at all but a jellied meat mixture based on either hog's head or pork shoulder. After mixing, chill the "cheese" in a pan and serve sliced. It is delicious and easy to make if you use the pork shoulder instead of the hog's head, but if you have access to a hog's head and would prefer to try that version, omit the pork shoulder and double all other ingredients in the recipe. Cook the cleaned head 4 to 5 hours in liquid.

Serve head cheese with thinly sliced red onion, chopped egg and Vinaigrette Sauce (*see* page 66).

## INGREDIENTS
4 Pounds pork shoulder
2 Carrots, scraped
1 Onion
4 Cloves
1 Bay leaf
A pinch each of thyme and sage
1 Small tongue
1 Pound veal (or leftover cooked chicken or ham)
3 Tablespoons gelatin
2 Tablespoons each lemon juice and sherry
Salt to taste
Coarsely ground black peppercorns

## EQUIPMENT
Sharp knife, loaf pans, cheesecloth, one 4-pound weight
(a brick wrapped twice in foil will do nicely)

## STEP ONE
# COOKING THE MEATS

**A.** Place pork, carrots, onion stuck with the cloves, bay leaf, thyme and sage in a large pot. Cover with water, bring to a boil, then lower heat and simmer for 1 hour.

**B.** Add the trimmed tongue and veal, and simmer for 1½ hours more, or until pork is well done and tender.

## STEP TWO
# CHOPPING THE MEATS

**A.** Remove the meats from the cooking liquid. Continue cooking the liquid while the meats cool.

**B.** Cut one-half the cooled pork, tongue and veal and/or leftover meats into ½-inch dice and coarsely chop the other half.

## STEP THREE
# COMBINING THE INGREDIENTS

**A.** Arrange the cubed and chopped meats in alternate layers in loaf pans.

**B.** Stir the gelatin, lemon juice and sherry into 6 cups hot stock until the gelatin is dissolved. Salt to taste.

**C.** Pour this stock over the meat to cover. Grind fresh black peppercorns liberally over the top.

**D.** Chill 2 hours, then cover with cheesecloth and wax paper and top with a 3–4 pound weight. Refrigerate 24 hours.

# RECIPES WITH SAUSAGE

# BUBBLE AND SQUEAK*

For a perfectly marvelous economy meal serve this old English favorite with mashed potatoes and a salad.
(Yield: 4 servings)

### INGREDIENTS
¾ Pound loose pork sausage meat
1 Small head cabbage
3 Cups White Sauce (*see* page 65)
1 or 2 Drops Tabasco
Dash garlic powder
1 Cup bread crumbs

## DIRECTIONS

**A.** Crumble sausage and fry to a golden brown.

**B.** Cut cabbage into eighths, discarding tough outer leaves and hard core, and boil in water to cover until tender; then drain and chop.

**C.** Meanwhile, prepare White Sauce as directed (see page 65). Adjust seasonings to taste and mix in Tabasco and garlic powder.

*The name comes from the squeaking sound the dish makes while it cooks.

**D.** Preheat oven to 250 degrees F.

**E.** Combine sausage and chopped cabbage in large casserole. Mix in white sauce and cover the top with bread crumbs.

**F.** Bake until sauce is hot and bubbly. Serve at once.

# TOAD IN THE HOLE

Another recipe from England, where they know how to treat a respectable sausage.

(Yield: 6 servings)

## INGREDIENTS

1½ Pounds loose pork sausage meat or pork sausages (*see* page 24)
5½ Tablespoons oil
1½ Cups all-purpose flour
½ Teaspoon baking powder
½ Teaspoon salt
2 Cups milk
2 Eggs, beaten
1 Pinch each of ground nutmeg, thyme and cayenne pepper
Currant jelly (optional)

## DIRECTIONS

**A.** Preheat oven to 375 degrees F.

---

**B.** Roll the loose sausage into 1-inch balls or cut the sausage links into 1-inch pieces. Brown these in 1½ tablespoons of the oil in a heavy skillet. Reserve the pan drippings.

---

**C.** Sift together the flour, baking powder and salt. Stir in the milk, eggs, remaining 4 tablespoons oil and spices.

**D.** Pour 3½ to 4 tablespoons of the pan drippings into a rectangular glass baking dish. Pour in batter and arrange sausage pieces attractively. Bake for 30 minutes, or until puffy and golden brown. Serve immediately with currant jelly on the side.

# POOR MAN'S PAELLA

Sausage, seafood, chicken and rice in the same dish? Yes, and absolutely delicious! Here the chopped clams and clam juice provide the fish flavor that normally comes from expensive seafood.

(Yield: 6 to 8 servings)

## INGREDIENTS

1 3½-pound chicken, cut in parts
1½ Pounds Homemade Polish-Style Sausage (*see* page 38), or other highly flavored sausage
3 Large onions, peeled
4 Tablespoons cooking oil
1¾ Cups long-grain rice
⅛ Teaspoon saffron or turmeric
⅛ Teaspoon each powdered thyme and coarsely ground black pepper
1½ Cups (or one 10¾-ounce can) chicken broth
1 Bottle (8 ounces) clam juice
1 Can (8 ounces) chopped clams
1¾ Cups fresh (or 1 10-ounce package frozen) peas
¼ Cup pimiento squares

## DIRECTIONS

**A.** Rinse chicken pieces and pat dry. Cut sausage in ¼-inch-thick slices. Cut onions into coarse dice. In a large heavy Dutch oven or skillet sauté the chicken pieces in the hot oil until lightly browned on all sides. Remove and set aside.

**B.** Fry sausage slices and onion in oil in pan until onion is transparent. Set aside with the chicken. Add uncooked rice to the pan and stir over medium heat for 5 minutes (add more oil if necessary to coat the rice). Stir in the spices.

**C.** Return the chicken and sausage to the pot. Add the chicken broth, clam juice and chopped clams. (Take care to spoon the clams and juice carefully into the pot so as not to disturb any sand that may be on the bottom of the can.) Add enough water to just cover the ingredients in the pot. Cover and bring to just under a boil. Lower heat and simmer, covered, for 15 minutes. Stir in the peas and pimiento, cover and simmer 15 to 20 minutes longer, or until rice tests done. Serve hot.

# ITALIAN SAUSAGE CASSEROLE

Sausages and green peppers, traditional "go-togethers," become an unbeatable combination when dotted with cubes of cheese, smothered in tomato sauce, topped with mashed potatoes and baked.

(Yield: 6 servings)

### INGREDIENTS

6 Green peppers with seeds, pith and stem removed
6 Italian-Style Sausages (*see* page 41) cut into 1-inch pieces
2 Tablespoons oil
¼ Pound piece of Cheddar Cheese
3 Cups tomato sauce
4 Cups mashed potatoes
3 Tablespoons milk
½ Teaspoon oregano
1 Clove garlic, peeled and crushed (optional)
¾ Cup grated Parmesan (or other) cheese

## DIRECTIONS

**A.** Preheat oven to 350 degrees F.

**B.** Fry peppers and sausage pieces in the oil, stirring frequently until the peppers are tender.

**C.** Arrange sausage and peppers in the bottom of a rectangular glass baking dish. Place the cheese cubes between the sausage pieces and pour the tomato sauce over all.

**D.** Beat together the mashed potatoes, milk, oregano and crushed garlic, season with salt to taste, and spoon dollops of the mixture evenly over the top of the sauce.

**E.** Sprinkle with Parmesan and bake for 40 minutes, or until top is golden brown. Serve immediately.

# SAUSAGE BAKED IN ITALIAN BREAD

An excellent way to feed a crowd inexpensively and well is to serve this spicy sausage and cheese loaf with a hearty soup, a salad and a very special dessert.

(Yield: 4 to 6 servings)

## INGREDIENTS

1 Large Italian bread
2 Medium onions, peeled and coarsely chopped
¾ Cup minced mushrooms
1 Sweet red pepper with seeds, pith and stem removed
2 Tablespoons oil
1½ Pounds loose pork sausage meat
1 Clove garlic, peeled and crushed
⅛ Teaspoon sage
¼ Teaspoon each oregano and thyme
¾ Cup grated Cheddar, Swiss or Jack cheese
1 Egg, beaten
¼ Cup heavy cream

## DIRECTIONS

**A.** Cut the top third of the bread off in one slice. Pull out the soft center portion of the bread, leaving a 1-inch shell. Reserve the soft bread pieces you pull out.

**B.** Sauté the onions, mushrooms and sweet peppers in the oil.

**C.** Force these sautéed vegetables, the sausage meat, soft bread pieces, garlic, sage, oregano and thyme through a grinder three times.

**D.** Preheat oven to 350 degrees F.

**E.** Mix the cheese, egg and cream in thoroughly with a wooden spoon and stuff the bread shell with the mixture.

**F.** Cover the stuffed bread with the top slice and wrap well in 2 thicknesses aluminum foil, set on baking sheet and bake for 1 hour. Open foil and allow loaf to brown during the last 15 minutes.

# DEEP-FRIED SAUSAGE PIES

These crusty little pies lend themselves well to a variety of fillings.

(Yield: 6 servings)

**INGREDIENTS**

1 Recipe, Pie Crust (*see* page 64)
Filling of your choice (*see* below)
Oil for frying

## DIRECTIONS

**A.** Prepare pie crust as directed and roll out to medium thickness. Cut into 6-inch squares.

---

**B.** Place 2 to 3 tablespoons of any of the fillings listed below on one corner of each square. Moisten edges of squares with water, then fold over diagonally and seal by pressing edges together with a fork.

---

**C.** Fry pies in hot oil until golden brown on both sides, turning once. Drain briefly on paper towels. Keep pies hot in oven as you fry them. Serve very hot.

# FILLINGS

## SAUSAGE AND POTATO FILLING

Boil 2 medium potatoes in their skins, then peel and cut into ⅓-inch cubes. Combine with 2 cups cooked and crumbled sausage and ¼ teaspoon sage. Bind with ½ cup heavy cream or White Sauce (*see* page 65).

## SAUSAGE AND EGG FILLING

Peel and chop 3 hard-cooked eggs. Trim and chop 2 scallions, including 3 inches green top. Combine scallions and eggs with 2 cups cooked and crumbled sausage. Season with pinch or two of dill and bind with ½ cup heavy cream or White Sauce (*see* page 65).

## VIENNA SAUSAGE FILLING

Peel and mince onion. Remove seeds, pith and stems from 1 green pepper; chop finely. Sauté onion and pepper in 1½ tablespoons butter until vegetables are soft. Combine with 2 cups minced Vienna sausage, ¼ cup ketchup, 2 tablespoons mild mustard, 2 tablespoons maple syrup and ⅛ teaspoon oregano.

# MIDWESTERN BOILED DINNER

Here's a robust family meal—lovely to look at, full of old-fashioned good flavor and cooked all in one pot! Fresh vegetables and Polish sausage combine for stick-to-the-ribs goodness.

(Yield: 8 servings)

## INGREDIENTS
2½ Pounds Homemade Polish-Style Sausage (see page 38)
2 Pounds new potatoes, washed
Salted water
12 Carrots, scraped
1 Pound fresh asparagus, trimmed
Salt and pepper

## DIRECTIONS

**A.** In large Dutch oven, place whole Polish sausage and new potatoes with water to cover. Cover and bring to a boil; reduce heat to simmer. Simmer 20 minutes, or until potatoes are almost done.

**B.** Add carrots and simmer, covered, for 10 minutes. Add asparagus and cook, covered, another 5 minutes. Drain. On large platter arrange the Polish sausage links in circles and fill the center with potatoes. Arrange carrots and asparagus in spoke fashion around sausage. Serve immediately.

# SAUSAGE AND POTATO SALAD

Center a summer lunch or supper around this unusually delicious potato salad. Season to your taste* and serve each portion on a crisp lettuce leaf. Garnish with thin slices of tomato, cucumber and hard-cooked egg.

(Yield: 6 servings)

## INGREDIENTS

5 Medium potatoes, boiled in their skins
¾ Cup dry white wine
1½ Pounds sausage links, cooked and cut into ¼-inch slices
5 Scallions, including 3 inches green top
3 Tablespoons tarragon or other mild vinegar
1 Tablespoon Dijon mustard
2 Tablespoons olive oil
Salt and freshly ground black pepper to taste

## DIRECTIONS

**A.** Peel potatoes and cut into ¼-inch slices.

**B.** Heat wine to wrist temperature and toss gently with potato and sausage slices. Marinate at room temperature for 1 hour.

*Add fresh sage or thyme if available and 1 teaspoon sugar if you prefer a sweet-tart flavor.

**C.** Mince scallions and add them, along with the remaining ingredients, to the marinated sliced potatoes and sausages. Toss gently. Serve at room temperature.

# PIE CRUST

(Yield: enough pastry for a double-crust pie)

### INGREDIENTS

2 Cups all-purpose flour
1 Teaspoon salt
12 Tablespoons vegetable shortening
6 to 8 Tablespoons ice water

## DIRECTIONS

**A.** Combine flour and salt. Sift together into large bowl.

---

**B.** Cut in shortening with two knives or pastry blender until mixture resembles coarse meal. Sprinkle with 6 tablespoons ice water, stir with a fork, then press into a firm ball. (If pastry crumbles, work in remaining ice water.) Chill 15 minutes.

---

**C.** Divide dough in half. Roll out each half on a lightly floured pastry board. Do not overwork the dough.

# WHITE SAUCE

(Yield: 2 cups)

### INGREDIENTS

4 Tablespoons butter
4 Tablespoons flour
½ Teaspoon salt
2 Cups cold milk*
White pepper

## DIRECTIONS

**A.** Melt butter over medium heat in a heavy saucepan or skillet. Add flour and salt and stir with a fork until smooth. Remove pan from heat.

**B.** Add milk all at once. Stir until mixture is well blended and lump-free.

**C.** Return pan to medium heat and cook, stirring constantly, until sauce is creamy and thick. Season with white pepper.

*Note: To make a thinner sauce, increase milk to 2½ cups. To make a thicker sauce, reduce amount of milk to 1¼ cups.

# VINAIGRETTE SAUCE

(Yield: about 1 cup)

### INGREDIENTS

6 Tablespoons wine vinegar
½ Teaspoon salt
Freshly ground black pepper
½ Teaspoon dry mustard (optional)
⅔ Cup olive or salad oil or combination
4 Tablespoons finely minced chervil, parsley or tarragon, singly
or in combination

## DIRECTIONS

**A.** Beat the vinegar with the salt, pepper and dry mustard until well blended. Add the oil and beat again.

---

**B.** Just before serving, mix the herbs into the dressing.

# THE PROCESS
# DESCRIBED

# CHOPPING OR GRINDING THE MEAT

You can prepare meats for sausagemaking in two ways:

**A.** **By hand.** Use a *very* sharp knife to cut the meat into ¼-inch dice. If you do not intend to freeze the sausages or patties, partially freeze the meat beforehand to make the chopping easier. This hand-chopping method is more tedious than machine-grinding but it produces superior sausages.

**B.** **With an electric or hand grinder.** For an interesting texture use only the large-holed, coarse disk of your grinder, unless otherwise specified in your recipe.

# MIXING THE INGREDIENTS

**A.** Mix all ingredients in a large bowl.

**B.** Distribute spices evenly by working or kneading the mixture with your fingers.

# PREPARING AND STORING THE CASINGS

**NATURAL CASINGS** are best, since you can eat them and since they stretch and shrink with the sausage. Usually available at fine butcher shops, these are packaged dry and salted and come in widths ranging from 1 to 4 inches. To prepare them for use, follow these steps:

**A.** Rinse approximately as much casing as you need at one time under running water. Soak in warm water for 30 minutes, changing the water several times.

**B.** Insert two fingers into one end of each casing to separate the sides. Hold the open end under running water. Allow the water to penetrate the length of the casing. If the casing has an inner membrane, remove it at this point.

**C.** Place the rinsed casings on paper towels until ready to stuff.

**D.** Rinse any unused casings and repack in salt in their original containers.

Natural casings packed in salt will keep for up to two years. To preserve them at peak quality . . .

**A.** Store in original containers in the refrigerator or freezer.

**B.** Sprinkle with additional table salt from time to time.

**MUSLIN CASINGS,** which you can cut to any size, are particularly handy for oversized sausages. They also take much of the guesswork out of the smoking process, since smoke colors the casing as well as the sausage and indicates when smoking is complete. To prepare muslin casings for use . . .

**A.** Tear plain unbleached muslin into strips slightly longer and wider than desired size. Fold in half lengthwise and press with iron at warm setting.

**B.** Mark the end of the folded strip opposite the selvage end with a semicircle, taking care to pencil only to within ¼-inch of the end of the cloth.

**C.** Begin at folded end and sew around the semicircle; then stitch tightly down open seam. Trim all loose threads and cut edges close with pinking shears.

**D.** Turn casing inside out and use.

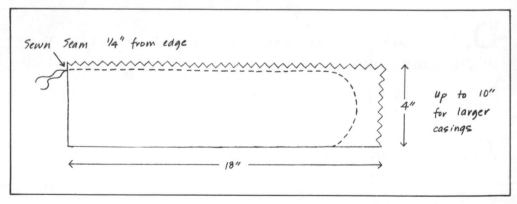

Sewn Seam   ¼" from edge

4"

Up to 10" for larger casings

18"

# SHAPING THE MEAT

**A.** To make sausage patties, shape the well-chilled meat mixture with your hands to desired size and thickness. Cover individual patties with plastic wrap or wax paper, then cover with suitable freezer wrap. Seal tightly. After wrapping, refrigerate and use within 3 days, or freeze at 0 degrees F. (*see* Storing Sausages, page 78).

**B.** To make a sausage roll, turn the well-chilled meat mixture onto a pastry board. Knead in 2 tablespoons of ice water, wrap, refrigerate and use within 2 to 3 days, or freeze at 0 degrees F.

# FILLING THE CASINGS

## USING FUNNEL AND SPOON:

**A.** Prepare casing as directed on page 71. While still wet, open one end and slip it over the spout of your funnel. Slide the remaining length of casing up onto the spout, in a sort of accordion pleat.

**B.** Hold funnel with casing attached in the crook of your left arm, against your body. (If left-handed, reverse these directions.)

**C.** Pack some of the sausage mixture into the funnel, tamping it down into the funnel spout with the handle of a wooden spoon. (Dip the spoon in ice water to keep sausage from sticking to it.)

**D.** As soon as the sausage mixture is flush with the tip of the funnel spout, pull about 1 inch of casing out and away and tie the casing off. (If the casing is tied before the sausage mixture is level with the tip of the spout, air in the funnel will cause the casing to inflate.)

**E.** Reposition the funnel under your arm. Keep your left thumb and forefinger on the casing and release it gradually as you force in the sausage mixture. Stuff the casing loosely; the filling expands when cooked. Tie off sausages the length you prefer.

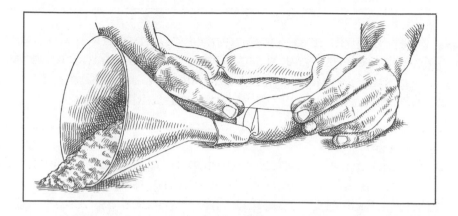

# USING AN ELECTRIC OR HAND SAUSAGE STUFFER

Special stuffing nozzles available for electric mixers and/or meat grinders make filling casings quick and easy.

**A.** Assemble sausage-stuffing equipment, following manufacturer's directions. Prepare casings as directed on page 71.

**B.** Slip the wet, open end of the casing over the outside of the stuffer tube. Slide remaining length of casing onto the tube spout.

**C.** To prevent air from being forced into casing ahead of sausage mixture, force some of the sausage mixture through the machine until it is flush with the end of the tube.

**D.** Pull about 1 inch of casing out and away from the spout and tie securely.

**E.** Keep thumb and forefinger of one hand on the casing to guide its release away from the mouth of the tube as it fills. Stop the stuffing action and tie off as desired. Do not overstuff, or casings will burst during cooking.

**F.** Should an air pocket develop in a sausage, pierce the casing with a large needle. If a casing tears, stop the machine and tie off the sausage. Then proceed as before.

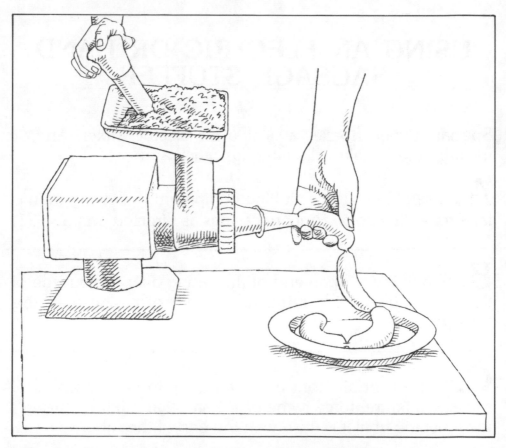

# TYING OFF

To tie off the stuffed casings, use one of two methods:

**A.** Twist the casing several turns as soon as each sausage reaches the desired length, *or*

**B.** Tie off with heavy thread or light string.

# SMOKING THE SAUSAGES

While many elaborately designed smoke ovens are available on the market, you can make a perfectly satisfactory and efficient smoker out of a covered barbecue, hibachi or other fireproof container of similar construction. All you need are the following items:
— a slow-burning hardwood fire to produce the smoke. Charcoal or briquets topped with sawdust may also be used.
— a cover for the smoker to confine the smoke to one area. Use either the top of a grill or barbecue, aluminum foil, or a tent of green branches.
— upper and lower air outlets. Most homemade—and therefore fairly drafty—smoke ovens allow easy circulation of air at both the top and bottom. If air circulation is impaired, the sausages tend to take on sooty, unwholesome odors.
— sturdy supports to hold the sausages during smoking. These may be a frame with hooks, Y-shaped sticks, or any other similar device designed so that smoke reaches all areas uniformly.

—a thermometer to gauge smoking temperatures. Smoke your sausages at temperatures of 60 degrees F. to 85 degrees F., or as indicated in your recipe.

# STORING SAUSAGES

As soon as you've prepared the sausage mixture and shaped it into patties or rolls or stuffed it into casings, treat the sausages as follows:

**A.** Cover or wrap tightly and refrigerate immediately. Use within 3 days.

**B.** To freeze, cover individual patties or rolls with plastic wrap or wax paper, then cover with freezer wrap. Seal tightly.

# COOKING THE SAUSAGE

## COOKING SAUSAGE LINKS

**A.** Homemade sausages are occasionally overstuffed. To avoid the inevitable "Pop!" of split casings, prick each sausage in 5 or 6 places with a sharp fork or needle before arranging them in the pan. This permits some juice and fat to escape during cooking and prevents build-up of pressure inside the casing.

**B.** Place sausages in a single layer in a pan just large enough to hold them without crowding.

**C.** Add enough water to reach halfway up the sausage sides.

**D.** Simmer covered for 5 minutes. Turn, re-cover and simmer 5 minutes longer.

**E.** Pour off the water and blot excess moisture with paper towels. Add 2 to 3 tablespoons vegetable oil to the pan and brown sausages on all sides over low heat. Pork should be eaten well done.

## COOKING SAUSAGE PATTIES

**A.** Heat a small amount of vegetable oil in a heavy skillet.

**B.** Brown patties well on both sides. Be sure meat is well done.

Yvonne Young Tarr is a veteran cookbook writer. Her books include *The Ten Minute Gourmet, The Ten Minute Gourmet Diet Cookbook, 101 Desserts to Make You Famous, Love Portions, The New York Times Natural Foods Dieting Book, The Complete Outdoor Cookbook, The New York Times Bread and Soup Cookbook, The Farmhouse Cookbook* and *The Up-with-Wholesome, Down-with-Storebought Book of Recipes and Household Formulas.*

She is married to sculptor William Tarr. They have two children, Jonathon and Nicolas.